FIRST EXPERIENCES

AMY'S FIRST AIRPLANE RIDE

by Katie Chanez
illustrated by Daniela Massironi

Tools for Parents & Teachers

Grasshopper Books enhance imagination and introduce the earliest readers to fiction with fun storylines and illustrations. The easy-to-read text supports early reading experiences with repetitive sentence patterns and sight words.

Before Reading

- Look at the cover illustration. What do readers see? What do they think the book will be about?
- Look at the picture glossary together. Sound out the words. Ask readers to identify the first letter of each vocabulary word.

During Reading

- "Walk" through the book with the reader. Discuss new or unfamiliar words. Sound them out together.
- Look at the pictures together. Point out any labels.

After Reading

- Review the picture glossary again. Ask readers to locate the words in the text.
- Ask the reader: How does Amy feel before flying? How does she feel after? How do you know?

Grasshopper Books are published by Jump!
3500 American Blvd W, Suite 150
Bloomington, MN 55431
www.jumplibrary.com

Jump! is a division of FlutterBee Education Group.

Library of Congress Cataloging-in-Publication Data

Names: Chanez, Katie, author.
Massironi, Daniela, illustrator.
Title: Amy's first airplane ride / by Katie Chanez; illustrated by Daniela Massironi.
Description: Minneapolis, MN: Jump!, Inc., 2026.
Series: First experiences
Audience: Ages 3–6.
Identifiers: LCCN 2024044264 (print)
LCCN 2024044265 (ebook)
ISBN 9798892138673 (hardcover)
ISBN 9798892138680 (paperback)
ISBN 9798892138697 (ebook)
Subjects: CYAC: Air travel—Fiction. | Emotions—Fiction.
Courage—Fiction. | LCGFT: Picture books.
Classification: LCC PZ7.1.C4794 Am 2026 (print)
LCC PZ7.1.C4794 (ebook)
DDC [E] —dc23
LC record available at https://lccn.loc.gov/2024044264
LC ebook record available at https://lccn.loc.gov/2024044265

Editor: Alyssa Sorenson
Direction and Layout: Molly Ballanger
Illustrator: Daniela Massironi

Printed in the United States of America at
Corporate Graphics in North Mankato, Minnesota.

Table of Contents

In the Air

It is my first time flying.

I am scared.

We get on the airplane.

My stomach hurts.

We find our seats.

Mom says, "Put your seat belt on, Amy."

seat belt

"What if something goes wrong?" I ask.

"The flight attendants teach us how to be safe," Dad says.

The airplane takes off.

It shakes.

Then it is smooth.

We are in the air!

I see clouds.

They bring snacks.

I watch a movie.

It is fun!

screen
snack

The airplane lands.

We are safe.

I am brave!

Let's Review!

Amy is scared to fly. How do we know?

A. She cries. **B.** She holds her mom and dad's hands.
C. She yells. **D.** Her stomach hurts.

Picture Glossary

brave
To have courage and face fear.

flight attendants
People who work on airplanes to help keep passengers safe and comfortable.

lands
Arrives on the ground after being in the air.

shakes
Moves quickly back and forth or up and down.

smooth
Without roughness or bumps.

takes off
Leaves the ground and begins flying.

Let's Review! Answer Key: **B.** She holds her mom and dad's hands. **D.** Her stomach hurts.